Dear Parent:

Congratulations! Your child is taking the first steps on an exciting journey. The destination? Independent reading.

STEP INTO READING® will help your child get there. The program offers books at five levels that accompany children from their first attempts at reading to reading success. Each step includes fun stories, fiction and nonfiction, and colorful art. There are also Step into Reading Sticker Books, Step into Reading Math Readers, and Step into Reading Phonics Readers— a complete literacy program with something to interest every child.

Learning to Read, Step by Step!

Ready to Read Preschool–Kindergarten
• big type and easy words • rhyme and rhythm • picture clues
For children who know the alphabet and are eager to begin reading.

Reading with Help Preschool–Grade 1
• basic vocabulary • short sentences • simple stories
For children who recognize familiar words and sound out new words with help.

Reading on Your Own Grades 1–3
• engaging characters • easy-to-follow plots • popular topics
For children who are ready to read on their own.

Reading Paragraphs Grades 2–3
• challenging vocabulary • short paragraphs • exciting stories
For newly independent readers who read simple sentences with confidence.

Ready for Chapters Grades 2–4
• chapters • longer paragraphs • full-color art
For children who want to take the plunge into chapter books but still like colorful pictures.

STEP INTO READING® is designed to give every child a successful reading experience. The grade levels are only guides. Children can progress through the steps at their own speed, developing confidence in their reading, no matter what their grade.

Remember, a lifetime love of reading starts with a single step!

To my sister Emma, who loves plants
—M.B.

For my daughters, Anna and Claire
—P.M.

Special thanks to Leo Song, Jr., Department of Biological Sciences
Greenhouse Complex, California State University; Barry Meyers-Rice,
Carnivorous Plant Newsletter; *and Charles Clarke, Hong Kong*
University of Science and Technology

www.stepintoreading.com

Educators and librarians, for a variety of teaching tools, visit us at
www.randomhouse.com/teachers

Library of Congress Cataloging-in-Publication Data
Batten, Mary.
Hungry plants / by Mary Batten ; illustrated by Paul Mirocha. — 1st Random House ed.
   p.   cm. — (Step into reading. A step 4 book)
SUMMARY: Describes the structure and behavior of various carnivorous plants, including the
Venus flytrap, sundew, pitcher plant, and bladderwort.
ISBN 0-375-82533-9 (trade) — ISBN 0-375-92533-3 (lib. bdg.)
1. Carnivorous plants—Juvenile literature. [1. Carnivorous plants.]
I. Mirocha, Paul, ill. II. Title. III. Series: Step into reading. Step 4 book.
QK917 .B38 2003 583'.75—dc21 2002014247

Printed in the United States of America 10 9 8 7 6 5 4 3 2 1
First Random House Edition

STEP INTO READING, RANDOM HOUSE, and the Random House colophon are registered trademarks of
Random House, Inc.

STEP INTO READING®

STEP 4

Hungry Plants

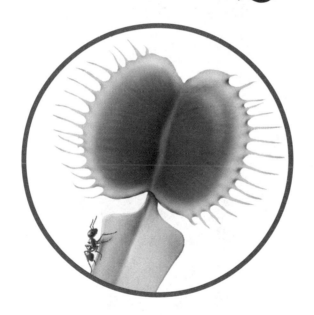

by Mary Batten

illustrated by Paul Mirocha

Random House 🏠 New York

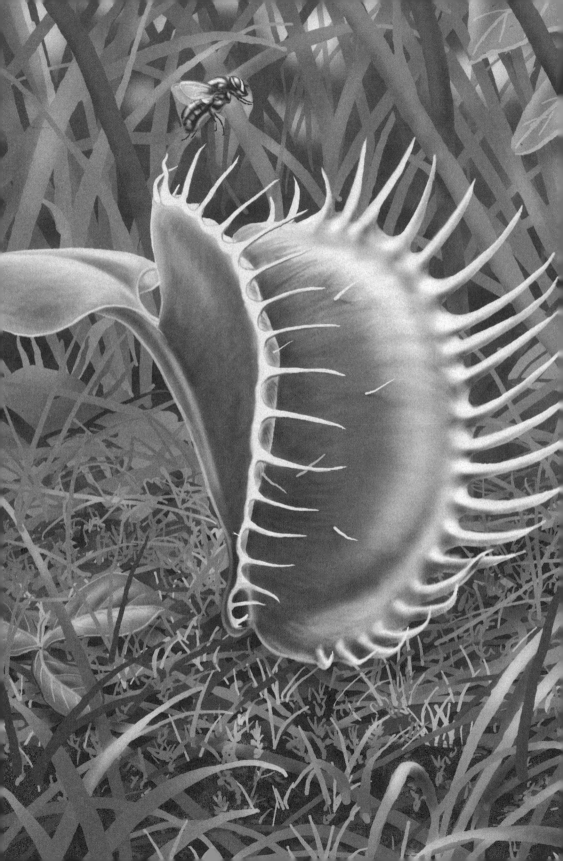

1. Gotcha!

Everything is quiet in the bog. Or *almost* everything.

A tiny black fly buzzes around, looking for food. All of a sudden, it smells nectar, a sugary juice that plants make. The sweet smell is coming from a strange plant growing flat against the ground.

The fly lands near the plant and crawls toward a leaf. Closer, closer, closer.

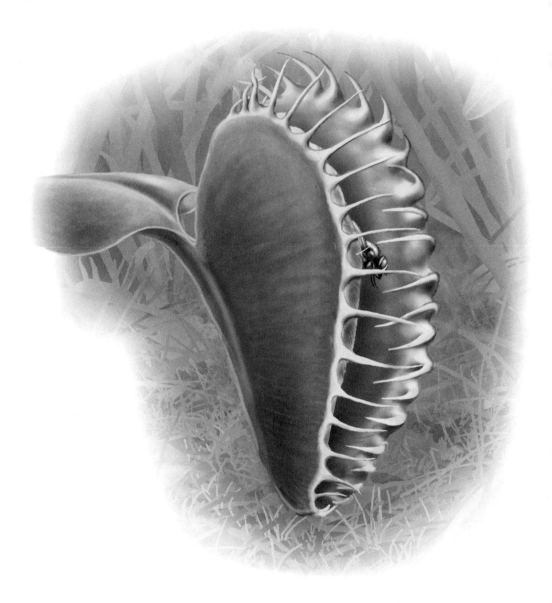

SNAP!

The leaf slams shut, squishing the fly between two green walls.

The fly tries to get out but can't. The fly will never escape. This plant will eat it alive!

How can a plant eat a fly?

It's easy for the Venus flytrap.

The Venus flytrap is just one of more than six hundred kinds of plants that eat insects and other tiny animals. These plants are called carnivorous (kar-NIV-ur-us). This word means "meat-eating." Carnivorous plants are the T. rexes of the plant world.

Eating bugs might seem like a strange thing for a plant to do. And it is. Most plants get everything they need to be healthy from sun, rain, and soil. But insect-eating plants grow in very poor soil. They make up for this by eating bugs. For these plants, eating bugs is like taking a vitamin pill.

Scientists say that insect-eating plants are very old. The first one appeared about sixty-five million years ago, around the time of the dinosaurs and long before there were any people on Earth.

We know about these old plants because just as there are dinosaur fossils, there are also plant fossils.

The oldest known carnivorous plant is Aldrovanda (al-dro-VAN-duh). Scientists have found fossils of its seeds.

Meat-eating plants hunt very differently than meat-eating animals.

Unlike animals, plants don't have legs. So they can't move around and hunt their prey like animals can. Plants don't have claws and sharp teeth either. But they can still catch food.

How do they do it?

With tricks and traps.

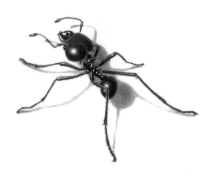

2. Gulp!

Carnivorous plants have different kinds of traps. Some, like the Venus flytrap, are active. This means that part of the plant moves to catch its meal. The Venus flytrap is active because its leaves snap shut.

The leaves of this meat-eating plant are really small traps with spines along the edges. Many traps are no larger than a dime. The biggest are about the size of a half-dollar. A Venus flytrap has about seven leaf traps.

On each leaf is a red spot. Insects like red, and they head toward it. The spot is covered with sweet nectar that lures the insect like fish to bait. But it's a trick. Instead of finding food, the insect *becomes* food for a hungry plant.

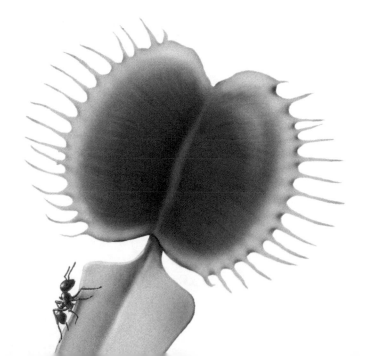

When a fly, or any other small insect, crawls onto a Venus flytrap leaf, it touches a tiny hair. Then the fly touches another tiny hair. These little hairs are triggers.

When two trigger hairs are touched or when one trigger hair is touched twice, the leaf trap suddenly snaps shut. The two sides of the leaf close around the insect. Like the bars of a cage, the spines keep the bug from escaping.

The Venus flytrap takes several days—sometimes as long as a week—to eat its food. The plant makes special juices that break down flies, spiders, ants, beetles, and any other bugs unlucky enough to get caught. The leaf will not open again until it is done with its meal.

Each Venus flytrap leaf can open and close about seven times. This means it can eat about seven insect meals. Then the leaf opens as wide as it can and just acts like a regular leaf. But the plant still has other leaf traps ready to catch its next victim.

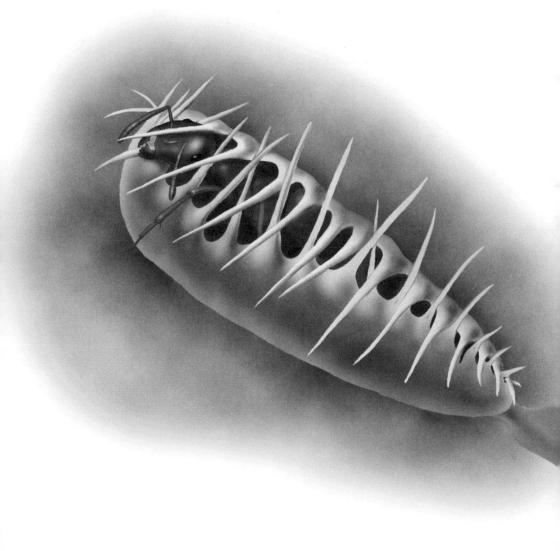

17

3. Slurp!

Another type of insect-eating plant is the bladderwort. It is also an active trap. There are more than two hundred kinds of bladderworts. Some have beautiful flowers that look like orchids. But quicker than you can blink your eye, bladderworts suck up their prey.

The bladderwort's traps are tiny pouches shaped like little eggs. Most bladderworts grow in ponds or lakes. The plant's stem and flower grow above the water, but the traps are underwater. When tiny water animals swim by, they touch a trigger hair on

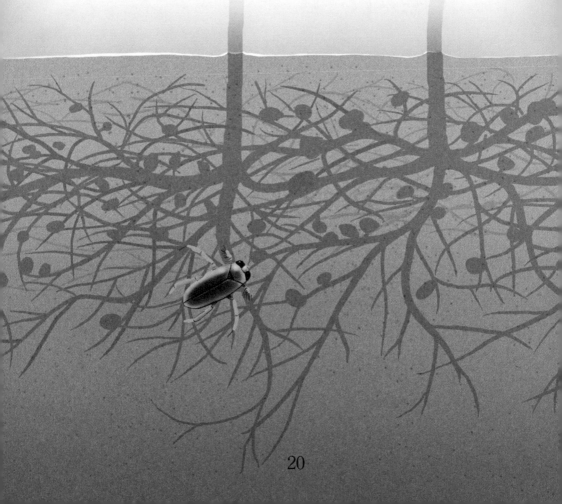

the plant's trapdoor. In less than half a second, the pouch opens, sucking the water and the animal inside—just as you'd suck juice through a straw. It takes about one hour for the plant to reset the trap. Then it's ready to catch another passing bug.

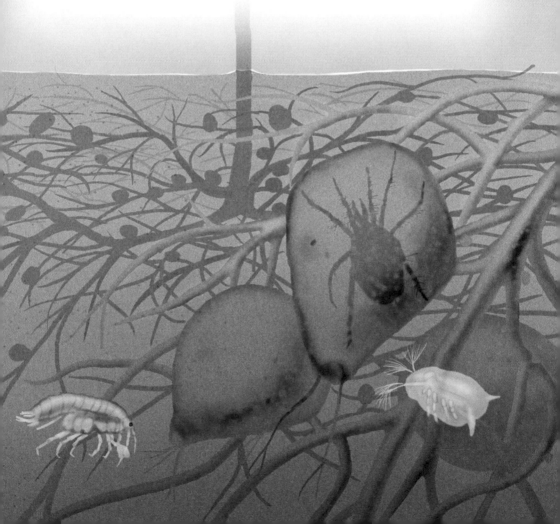

4. Slip and Slide

Like a small helicopter, a bee whizzes in for a landing on the edge of a plant. The bee smells nectar and wants a sip. It crawls inside the plant and quickly loses its footing. The plant walls are slippery.

The bee begins to slide. It tries as hard as it can to climb out, but tiny downward-pointing hairs keep it from crawling back up. Down, down, down the bee slides. It can't stop. At the bottom of the plant is a pool of water.

SPLASH! The bee falls in. It can't get out. Soon the bee drowns. Then chemicals in the water help the plant digest the bee just as chemicals inside your stomach help you digest your food.

The unlucky bee fell into a pitcher plant, another kind of carnivorous plant. Unlike Venus flytraps and bladderworts, pitcher plants don't move. So they are called passive traps.

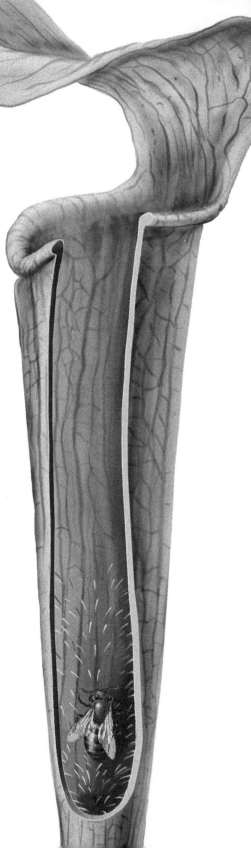

They, too, use nectar to bait insects. But they just sit still and wait for their victims to fall inside.

There are many different kinds of pitcher plants. Some grow on long vines in tropical countries where it is hot all year round. Many tropical pitcher plants grow in rainforests on mountains thousands of feet high.

Borneo is home to the biggest, most spectacular pitcher plants in the world. Some have stems more than sixty feet long that snake along the ground or hang from trees. Some are big enough to trap a tree frog or a small bird. Others are so tiny they can't catch anything larger than an ant.

Tropical pitcher plants look like hanging pouches. The plant's "pitcher" is really a leaf that grows in an unusual shape. The opening is the pitcher's mouth. The pouch is its stomach.

Most tropical pitcher plants are climbing vines that usually have two types of pitchers. Lower pitchers are shaped sort of like cans. Because they are closer to the ground, lower pitchers catch crawling insects. Upper pitchers are shaped like funnels. Upper pitchers catch mostly flying insects such as honeybees, flies, and hornets.

Above the plant's mouth is a hood that acts like a little umbrella. It keeps the pitcher from filling up with rainwater. Flying insects use the hood as a landing pad.

The pitcher doesn't always get a chance to eat every bug it catches.

Sometimes it is robbed by a food thief. A diving spider can dive into the pitcher and steal a bug the plant has trapped. Diving spiders can get out of pitcher plants without being trapped.

They crawl up a silk thread that they spin from their bodies. The thread acts like a safety line.

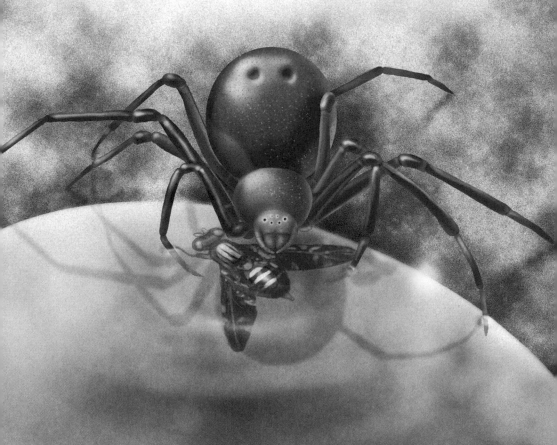

In the southern United States, pitcher plants grow in wet swampy places called pitcher plant bogs. They look very different from tropical

pitcher plants. These pitcher plants
don't hang from trees or cliffs.
Instead, they look like trumpets
growing out of the ground. In
Alabama, where many pitcher plants
grow, people call them "bug catchers."

These pitcher plants come in all
sorts of different sizes and colors. The
purple pitcher plant is one of the most
widespread insect-eating plants. It
has some silly nicknames: huntsman's
cap, sidesaddle pitcher plant, and
frog's britches.

The parrot pitcher plant has been
known to catch green tree toads and
chameleon lizards.

This pitcher plant grows in Oregon and California. It is called the cobra lily. Can you guess how it got its name?

The plant looks like a snake's head. It even has two flaps that look like fangs. The fangs make nectar.

Insects land on the fangs and then crawl inside the plant. But the cobra lily has a trick in store for its victims. It has fake light spots on the roof of its hood. Insects inside the plant see the spots and think there is a way out. But when the insect tries to escape by flying to the light, it crashes head-on into the plant's wall. Down it falls into the water-filled trap.

With all these tricks—light spots, hoods, pointy hairs, slippery sides— you'd think every bug would want to stay away from pitcher plants. But some bugs actually live inside them!

In fact, the water in pitcher plants is a perfect place for a mosquito to lay her eggs. When the eggs hatch, the young wormlike animals called larvae (LAR-vee) live in the water. The larvae are so small, they could fit in this letter **O**. No one knows why, but the pitcher plant does not eat them. So even pitcher plants can be a home for somebody.

5. Sticky Fingers

Sundews are some of the prettiest bug-eating plants around. But don't let that fool you. They are also pretty deadly.

Each sundew has tentacles that grow on its leaves. Sundews get their name from the little gluey balls that look like dewdrops on their tentacles.

When a beetle flies over the plant, it smells the plant's nectar and lands to take a sip. Then it gets stuck to the gooey balls. The beetle tries to pull its legs free. But it's no use. The harder the beetle tries to escape, the more glue the sundew makes.

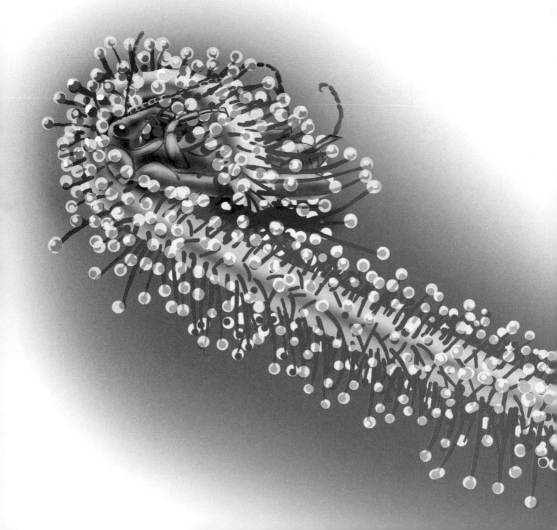

Then this passive trap becomes very active. The sticky tentacles slowly wrap around the insect's body, squeezing it so hard that it can't breathe. The sundew's tentacles make an acid that turns the beetle into beetle juice. The plant feeds on its "insect slurpy" for several days.

Sundews come in all sizes. The pygmy sundew is no bigger than a penny. The staghorn sundew may have as many as twelve branches and spread two feet across. It can catch larger bugs, like butterflies and moths.

Long ago, people believed that sundews could cure sickness. Many medicines were made from sundews. Mashed or chewed leaves were rubbed on warts, corns, and sunburns. Juices or teas made from the leaves were used to treat different diseases and problems such as asthma, whooping cough, and even toothaches. Some doctors today think that as a cough medicine, this old home remedy really works!

The great British scientist Charles Darwin was fascinated by sundews. He thought they had a stronger sense of taste and touch than any animal he had studied. Darwin spent twenty years studying insect-eating plants. In 1875, he wrote an entire book about them.

6. Hungry Plants and You

Some of these plants seem pretty scary. But can a meat-eating plant hurt a person?

No. The traps of most carnivorous plants are very small. Even the largest—on the monkey pot pitcher plant—are no bigger than a football. The biggest animal ever found in a monkey pot pitcher plant was a rat.

The rat may have been sick or
weak because a healthy rat could easily
claw its way out of a pitcher plant.

So there's nothing for you to worry about. You could crush most carnivorous plants under your foot. But please don't!

Some of these plants are endangered, just like certain animals. The bogs and wetlands where many of these plants live are being cleared for farms and houses. In other places, pollution from fertilizers and pesticides poisons the soil and kills the plants.

Venus flytraps are now extremely rare. They grow wild in only one place in the entire world—a narrow strip of land just ten miles wide and one hundred miles long on the coasts of North and South Carolina. It is against the law to pick wild Venus flytraps. Poachers who get caught have to pay a large fine.

Just as zoos try to save endangered animals, botanical gardens try to save endangered plants. They collect seeds and grow Venus flytraps, sundews, pitcher plants, and bladderworts.

If you want to see a hungry plant
in action, try going to a botanical
garden. Many have whole displays of
insect-eating plants.

Or you can even try growing a carnivorous plant at home. Just let it catch its own buggy snacks. Some people try to help by feeding their plants hamburger. That's a mistake. It can kill the plant! All the plant's energy is used up digesting the hamburger.

Remember—the only kind of fast food these plants eat is the kind that flies.

SNAP!